# International Food Library

# FOOD IN
# ITALY

# International Food Library

# FOOD IN ITALY

## Claudia Gaspari

**Rourke Publications, Inc.**
**Vero Beach, Florida 32964**

## Library of Congress Cataloging-in-Publication Data

Gaspari, Claudia, 1930-
    Food in Italy/by Claudia Gaspari.
       p. cm. - (International food)
    Includes index.
    Summary: Surveys food products, customs, and preparation in Italy, describing regional dishes, cooking techniques, and recipes for a variety of meals.
    ISBN 0-86625-342-4
    1. Cookery, Italian - Juvenile literature. 2. Food habits - Italy - Juvenile literature. 3. Italy - Social life and customs - Juvenile literature. [1. Cookery, Italian. 2. Food habits - Italy.
3. Italy - Social life and customs.] I. Title. II. Series.
International food series.
TX723.G285   1989
394. 1'0945-dc19        88-33269
                      CIP
                      AC

# CONTENTS

# AN INTRODUCTION TO ITALY

The Republic of Italy lies in southern Europe, bordered on three sides by sea. The main part of the peninsula is about 700 miles long and a little over 100 miles wide from coast to coast. The broad sweep of the Alps mountain ranges runs the length of Italy's eastern and northern borders and divides it from its neighbors: France to the west, and Switzerland and Austria to the north.

Italy also owns the two large islands of Sardinia and Sicily, as well as several small islands in the Tyrrhenian and Mediterranean Seas. Italy has two independent states within its borders. The sovereign republic of San Marino, a tiny landlocked area, lies in the northeast, close to the town of Rimini. The even smaller sovereign state of Vatican City, the center of the Roman Catholic religion, is in Rome.

**The Coliseum in Rome is a stunning example of early Roman architecture.**

**ITALY**

Milan

Venice

River Po

Parma

Genoa

Bologna

SAN MARINO

CORSICA

Rome

Naples ● △ Mt. Vesuvius

PUGLIA

SARDINIA

TYRRHENIAN SEA

Mt. Stromboli △

Mt. Etna △

SICILY

Rome, the capital and the most important center politically and economically, is the largest city in Italy. It was, of course, the hub of the Roman Empire when it dominated Europe and North Africa during the first to third centuries A.D. The city still boasts the best examples of Roman architecture with its famous Coliseum and Forum.

Italy is a mountainous country. A ridge of mountains, the Apennines, cuts the country in half lengthwise, leaving rolling coastal plains on either side. Italy has three volcanos, Mount Etna, Mount Vesuvius, and Mount Stromboli, which is on an island off the southwest coast. The most famous of these is Mount Vesuvius, which erupted in 70 A.D. and totally buried the city of Pompeii. This fine city, preserved by the volcanic rock, has been excavated by archaeologists and presents a very precise picture of how people lived in Roman times.

# AGRICULTURE IN ITALY

Since the 1930s, when over half the population was engaged in agriculture, Italy has developed into a strong industrial nation. Today, only 12 percent of the total work force is employed in the agricultural sector. Italy has over 3 million farms, most of which are privately owned and small by today's standards. Each averages less than 20 acres. Even though industry now dominates the economy, agricultural produce still accounts for nearly one-fifth of Italy's total exports.

Italy's agriculture is divided between two principal areas that are very different from one another. The northern agricultural region is the larger of the two, occupying almost one-fifth of Italy's land area. It spreads along the flat plains of the Po River, which rises in the western Alps and flows westward to the Gulf of Venice.

**Vegetables are cultivated in many parts of Italy. This picture shows the basilica of St. Francis of Assisi in the background.**

**The landscape of Tuscany is full of vineyards like this one near Florence.**

The Po Basin, as it is called, produces most of Italy's wheat, corn, rice, hemp, sugar beet, and grapevines, and is the center for livestock and dairy farming. The farms are highly mechanized, efficient, and well organized. This region produces 40 percent of Italy's total agricultural output, even though less than 25 percent of its working population are involved in farming.

The other principal growing region is in the far southeast of the country. In the plains of Puglia, over half the population is dependent on agriculture, whether as farmers, transporters, or suppliers of goods and services to the farm. The soil is less fertile, and the farms are generally smaller and less developed than those in the Po Basin. In Puglia the main crops are typically Mediterranean: olives, fruit, vegetables, and vines.

# FOOD IN ITALY

Italy is famous for its pasta, pizzas, and ice cream, but it is the home of many other fine foods as well. The country's dairies produce a whole range of cheeses, such as mozzarella, gorgonzola, ricotta, and parmigiano. Italy's meat products are exported internationally: prosciutto ham and all sorts of sausages and salamis find their way to homes and restaurants throughout the world. For those with a sweet tooth, Italian chocolates and confectionery are among the best in Europe.

In Italy, pasta and pizzas form an important part of a main meal. Since potatoes have never been as popular as they are in other European countries, pasta and pizza dishes generally provide the starch in the Italian diet. They are normally served as a separate second or third course.

There are well over one hundred varieties of pasta, and an inexhaustible list of pasta recipes. They are all made in essentially the same way, but are different shapes and sizes. The best known kinds are spaghetti, macaroni, canelloni, lasagne, vermicelli, and tagliatelle, all of which can be bought in any grocery store or

**Pasta in all shapes and sizes is served with many kinds of sauces.**

**Parma ham is one of Italy's prized exports.**

supermarket. Pizzas, too, vary in shape and size, and toppings can be anything from plain tomato sauce to a full complement of cheese, tomato, onion, mushroom, peppers, and tuna or pepperoni. In fact, anything goes!

Italian meals are usually hearty, consisting of at least three courses for a light lunch or supper and six or seven for a more formal occasion. These include hors d'oeuvres, soup, a rice or pasta dish, fish or meat, salad or vegetables, cheese and fruit, and dessert with coffee. All this, of course, is taken at a slow pace, with plenty of conversation and Italian wine to help it along.

# OLIVES

The hot dry summers and cool winters of southern Europe are excellent for cultivating olives. Europe produces three-quarters of the world's olives, with Italy the second largest producer after Spain. Italian olives, grown mainly in southern Italy and on the islands of Sicily and Sardinia, account for around one-fifth of global output.

Olives have been an important crop in Italy since Roman times; the records show them to have been cultivated since 600 B.C. They were probably introduced by the Greeks, who had by that time been growing olives for almost three thousand years.

**Olive trees are common in Mediterranean countries; this picture shows an olive grove in southern Italy.**

**Olives are often served as hors d'oeuvres, either on their own or as a garnish.**

The bushy and often gnarled olive trees are a familiar sight in southern Mediterranean countries. They grow slowly, but are extremely hardy and live for a very long time. Some trees are said to be over a thousand years old. In dry areas olive trees can take forty to fifty years to fully mature, although most will begin to bear fruit when they are between four and eight years old.

In late spring, the olive trees grow small white blossoms that develop into the olive fruits. By the fall the fruits are ready to be harvested for pickling in lye, a salty brine. These are sold as table olives. Nearly all the olives grown in Italy, however, are processed into olive oil and must be harvested later. They are left on the trees for six or eight months until they are fat and juicy with oil. Then they are harvested, usually by hand, and the oil is extracted in one of the many local factories. Olive oil is one of Italy's most important agricultural exports.

13

# DAIRY FARMING

Most of Italy's dairy farming is based in the four northern regions of Piedmont, Lombardy, Veneto, and Emilia-Romagna. Together, these regions contain around 70 percent of the country's total dairy herd of over 3 million, and produce about 80 percent of Italy's milk. Italy's southern regions, Puglia and Campania, also have a large number of large dairy farms and cheese factories.

Only around one-third of Italy's milk is processed and sold as milk. As a member of the European Economic Community, Italy is subject to a policy that limits the amount of milk it is allowed to produce. The country is supposed to import milk from north European dairies rather than produce its own, so that whatever is produced in the Community is used rather than wasted. This policy has caused problems for Italy's

**Parmigiano cheese is left to mature like this for eighteen months.**

**Parmigiano is one of Italy's most famous cheeses.**

dairy farmers, who are fined if they produce more milk than they are allowed to under the regulations. The Italian government has introduced grants to help the dairy farmers change to different kinds of farming.

Of the remaining milk, almost 90 percent is made into cheese, and 10 percent into butter. One of Italy's most famous cheeses, parmigiano, comes originally from Emilia-Romagna, where it has been hand-made for seven hundred years. Parmigiano takes nearly one month to make, and it must then be left to mature for eighteen months. The region of Campania is the home of another well-known cheese, mozzarella, which is made from water buffalos' milk. Italy exports over 30,000 tons of cheese each year, which accounts for one-quarter of the country's total agricultural export.

# REGIONAL COOKING

Since Italians only like to use the freshest local ingredients, each region has its own individual cuisine. An Italian would never consider preparing fish unless he or she was able to buy it fresh at the port, and the serious chef always uses vegetables that are home-grown.

**Basil, garlic, pine nuts, and olive oil are pounded together to make pesto.**

**Fresh fish is readily available in Italy's ports.**

Specialties from Italy's northern and central regions are often made from the abundant supply of meat and dairy produce. The city of Bologna is famous for sausages, particularly its mortadello sausage. Not far from Bologna lies the town of Parma, which has two very well known products: delicious, home cured parma ham and parmigiano cheese. Of course, all of these are prized ingredients in the local kitchens.

The old, picturesque ports of Genoa and Venice have made their own distinctive contributions to Italian cuisine. Genoa is the home of *pesto*, made from basil, garlic, and pine nuts pounded in olive oil. This simple yet subtle sauce is often used to flavor pasta. Venice, on the northeast coast, benefits from its historic trading relations with the east. Spices brought back from China and India by Marco Polo play an interesting part in Venetian cooking.

Southern cuisine is still spicier, with chilies and garlic adding zest to pasta, fish, and pizzas. Local vegetables such as the famous Italian plum-shaped tomatoes find their way into most southern dishes. Naples is famous as the home of pizzas and has some of the best seafood in all of Italy. The islands of Sicily and Sardinia, too, have their specialties. Sicily produces delicious sweets and pastries from ancient recipes passed on by the Arabs who once lived there, while Sardinia, as one may guess from its name, is famous for its sardines.

# ITALIAN FESTIVALS

Italians love to gather together for large family celebrations with music, dancing, lively conversation, and, of course, plenty of food and drink. In this predominantly Catholic country, most of the festivals are religious, and all are steeped in tradition.

One of the principal religious holidays is Epiphany, sometimes called Twelfth Night, which falls on January 6. This is the time when Italians give presents, usually to the children of the family. The Italian version of Santa Claus is the *Befana*, an old peasant woman who arrives on a donkey and climbs down chimneys to leave treats for the children. Much as we leave cookies and milk for Santa Claus, Italians leave some supper for the *Befana* and a carrot or an apple for her donkey.

As in many Christian countries, Italians observe the period of Lent, which begins on Ash Wednesday and ends on Palm Sunday. It marks the forty days and forty nights that Jesus spent in the wilderness, resisting all temptations. During Lent, many Catholics give up something they like to eat to remind themselves to resist temptation as Jesus did. Shrove Tuesday, the day before Lent begins, is a day of celebration called Carnival Day. It is a day for playing practical jokes, for parties, and for eating all those things that will be given up for the next forty days. Many cities throw street parties, where people old and young dress up in costumes and celebrate well into the night.

**Carnival Day costumes are often very spectacular.**

# A BANQUET MENU FOR A FESTIVE OCCASION

*Tuna And Bean Salad*
*Stracciatella*
*Chicken Risotto*
*Zucchini With Parmigiano*
*Almond Ice Cream*
*A Selection Of Fresh Fruit And Italian Cheeses*

Festive meals in Italy are always long and drawn out. Each course is served separately, although you may, if you prefer, serve the zucchini and the chicken risotto together. End the meal with a plate of fresh fruit in season and a selection of cheeses, such as gorgonzola, bel paese, fontina, and parmigiano.

## *Tuna And Bean Salad*

    1 small can tuna
    1 can cannellini beans
    1 onion, cut into rings
    1 teaspoon fresh basil, chopped
        pinch salt and black pepper
    2 tablespoons olive oil
    1 tablespoon wine vinegar

1. Mix all the ingredients together and leave to chill in the refrigerator. Serve cold.

**Stracciatella.**

**Chicken Risotto.**

### *Stracciatella*

> 6 *cups chicken stock*
> 3 *eggs*
> 4 *tablespoons white breadcrumbs*
> ½ *cup grated parmigiano*
> *pinch salt and black pepper*

1. Bring the stock to a boil and simmer while beating together the eggs, breadcrumbs and parmigiano in a bowl.
2. Pour a little of the stock in with the egg mixture, then stir it into the stock in the pan. Add the salt and pepper, simmer the soup for 1 minute, then serve immediately.

### Chicken Risotto

1½ lbs. boned chicken breast,
    cut into 1 inch cubes
6 slices bacon, finely chopped or minced
2 onions, chopped
2 sticks celery, chopped
1 can tomatoes, chopped
2 tablespoons olive oil
2 cups chicken stock
½ cup dry white wine
3 cups uncooked rice
1 bay leaf
1 teaspoon salt
½ teaspoon black pepper

1. Heat the oil in a large pan and gently fry the onion and celery for 2 minutes until soft. Add the chicken and bacon and fry for 5 minutes until lightly browned.
2. Add the tomatoes, bay leaf, salt, and pepper. Stir in the wine and cook for 5 minutes.
3. Add the rice and a little stock and bring to a boil. Simmer for 20 minutes, adding the stock a little at a time as the rice dries out. Garnish with parsley and serve hot.

### Zucchini With Parmigiano

1 lb. zucchini, sliced
1 onion, chopped
½ teaspoon minced garlic
2 tablespoons olive oil
4 tablespoons parmigiano
    pinch salt and black pepper

1. Heat the oil in a large pan and gently fry the onion and garlic for 2 minutes until soft.
2. Add the sliced zucchini, salt, and pepper. Cover the pan and cook for 10 to 15 minutes more until the zucchini is soft. Sprinkle with the parmigiano and serve hot.

**Zucchini With Parmigiano.**

### *Almond Ice Cream*

1¾ cups sugar
4 egg yolks
4 cups milk
1 teaspoon almond essence
½ cup flaked almonds

1. Beat together sugar and egg yolks in a pan over a low heat until smooth.
2. In another pan boil the milk. Add the hot milk to the sugar and egg mixture a little at a time, stirring constantly until you have a smooth, creamy custard. Do not boil the mixture. Remove from the heat.
3. Add the almonds and almond essence and then pour the mixture into six small freezer-proof dessert bowls and leave to cool. Freeze for 4 hours. Serve straight from the freezer.

# A MEAL FROM THE LOMBARDY REGION

*Osso Buco*
*Vegetable Risotto*
*Gorgonzola Cheese*

Osso buco is a well loved dish made from veal, which is plentiful in the northern regions of Italy. Serve it with vegetable risotto, and end the meal with crusty bread and gorgonzola cheese. In osso buco, wine is used to flavor the dish. It is cooked long enough so the alcoholic content disappears, but if you cannot use wine, try substituting a non-alcoholic wine, available in many supermarkets.

**Osso Buco.**

### Osso Buco

*1½ lbs. shank of veal, cut into 1 inch cubes*
*1 onion, chopped*
*2 tablespoons olive oil*
*1 teaspoon minced garlic*
*1 teaspoon salt*
*½ teaspoon black pepper*
*2 teaspoons fresh basil, finely chopped*
*1 cup dry white wine*

1. Heat the oil in a large pan and gently fry the onion and garlic for 2 minutes. Add the veal and fry for 10 minutes until lightly browned.
2. Add the wine, and simmer until most of the wine has evaporated and the sauce thickens slightly. Serve hot with the vegetable risotto.

### Vegetable Risotto

*1 cup uncooked rice*
*1 onion, finely chopped*
*1 cup green peas, canned or frozen*
*1 cup cooked borlotti beans*
*1 cup zucchini, sliced*
*1 can tomatoes, chopped*
*2 tablespoons olive oil*
*1 teaspoon salt*
*½ teaspoon black pepper*
*¼ cup grated parmigiano*
*2 cups chicken stock*

1. Heat the oil in a large pan and gently fry the onion for 2 minutes. Stir in the tomatoes, salt, and pepper, then add the rice and stock, and cook for 10 minutes.
2. Add the peas, beans, and zucchini and cook for 10 more minutes. If the rice looks dry add a little water, but do not make it too wet.
3. When the rice is soft and ready to eat, stir in the parmigiano and serve hot.

# A MEAL FROM THE CAMPANIA REGION

*Pizza Napoletana*
*Halibut With Tomato*
*Green Salad*

An authentic Neapolitan pizza (from Naples) is a treat not to be missed. Serve it as a first course, followed by the fish and a large bowl of green salad.

Pizzas can have a variety of toppings; this one adds leeks, baby onions and mushrooms to a standard cheese and tomato topping.

### Pizza Napoletana

    1 tablespoon yeast
    1 cup flour
      pinch salt
    3 medium tomatoes, chopped
    1 cup mozzarella cheese, grated
    3 anchovies
    ½ teaspoon oregano
    ½ teaspoon salt
    1 tablespoon olive oil

1. Make the pizza dough by dissolving the yeast in a cup of lukewarm water. Add ¼ cup flour and allow the mixture to rise.
2. Place the remaining flour and salt in a bowl and stir in the yeast mixture a little at a time to make a thick dough. If necessary add a little warm water to make the dough workable but not wet. Knead the dough for 5 minutes, then let rise. This will take 2 to 2½ hours.

3. When the dough has doubled in size, roll it out into a round shape and place it on a greased baking tray. Arrange the tomatoes, cheese, and anchovies on top. Sprinkle with oregano, salt, and olive oil, and bake in an oven preheated to 475 degrees for 15 minutes. When baked, cut into four pieces and serve hot.

### *Halibut With Tomato*

1½ lbs. halibut or other white fish fillets
6 tablespoons olive oil
1 onion, sliced
2 tablespoons tomato puree
1 teaspoon fresh basil, finely chopped
½ teaspoon salt
½ teaspoon black pepper
¼ cup flour
¼ cup water

1. Dip the fish fillets in the flour to coat them, and fry gently in oil in a large pan for 5 minutes. Remove the fish and put to one side.
2. Add the onion and basil to the pan and fry for 2 minutes. Stir in the tomato puree, water, salt, and pepper.
3. Place the fish back in the pan and simmer in the sauce for 15 minutes. Serve hot.

### *Green Salad*

½ head lettuce
1 cup watercress
½ cucumber, sliced
4 shallots, chopped
¼ cup olive oil
¼ cup vinegar

1. Mix together the lettuce, watercress, cucumber and shallots in a large salad bowl.
2. Mix together the olive oil and vinegar in a small jug to make a salad dressing.
3. Serve the salad and dressing together with the fish dish.

# AN EVERYDAY MEAL

Although not usually served in Italy as a complete meal in itself, spaghetti bolognese makes a nourishing and satisfying lunch for four people.

**Spaghetti Bolognese.**

### Spaghetti Bolognese

1½ lbs. ground beef
  1 large onion, chopped
  2 sticks celery, chopped
  1 teaspoon minced garlic
  1 teaspoon fresh or dried basil
  2 cans Italian plum tomatoes, chopped
  2 tablespoons tomato paste
  1 teaspoon salt
  1 teaspoon freshly ground black pepper
  1 tablespoon olive oil
 12 ozs. spaghetti
  ¼ cup parmigiano, grated

1. Heat the oil in a large saucepan and gently fry the onion, celery, and garlic for 3 minutes. Add the ground beef and fry for 5 minutes or until the meat is cooked.
2. Add the tomatoes, tomato paste, basil, salt, and pepper, and simmer for 20 minutes.
3. Bring a saucepan of salted water to a boil. Carefully add the spaghetti a little at a time, winding it around the inside of the pan as it softens in the boiling water. Simmer for 15 to 20 minutes, depending on the instructions given on the package.
4. When cooked, drain the spaghetti and divide between four serving dishes. Place the bolognese sauce on top and serve hot with a green salad. Serve the parmigiano in a small bowl with a spoon, and let each person sprinkle some on top of the sauce.

# GLOSSARY OF COOKING TERMS

*For those readers who are less experienced in the kitchen, the following list explains the cooking terms used in this book.*

| | |
|---|---|
| Boned | Having had the bones removed |
| Chopped | Cut into small pieces measuring about ½ inch |
| Finely chopped | Cut into very small pieces measuring about ⅛ inch |
| Garnished | Decorated |
| Greased | Having been lightly coated with oil or margarine to prevent the contents from sticking |
| Knead | To work a dough with one's hands |
| Minced | Chopped into tiny pieces or put through a mincer |
| Pinch | The amount you can pick up between your thumb and forefinger |
| Preheated | Alrady heated to the required temperature |
| Shelled | Having had the shells removed |
| Simmer | The lowest setting on a stove, usually marked |
| Sliced | Cut into pieces that show part of the original shape of the vegetable |
| Spoon measurements | Tablespoons and teaspoons should be filled only to the level of the spoon's edge, not heaped |

# ITALIAN COOKING

To make the recipes in this book, you will need the following special ingredients:

**Anchovies**  Anchovy fillets preserved in oil can be bought in tins from most large supermarkets.

**Borlotti beans**  Many different kinds of beans can be bought in cans. If you cannot find borlotti beans, use cannellini or butter beans.

**Cooking Wine**  Sold in supermarkets, especially to use in cooking.

**Herbs**  Basil, bay leaves, and oregano are all best when used fresh. Look for fresh herbs at a farmers' market or in the produce section of your supermarket.

**Mozzarella cheese**  Mozzarella is one of the more readily available Italian cheeses, and can be bought at any supermarket.

**Oil**  Butter and olive oil are most often used in Italian cooking, although olive oil is probably a better choice. It is cholesterol free, and therefore not only suitable for someone on a low-cholesterol diet but also healthier for you.

**Parmigiano**  If possible, this cheese, also called Parmesan, should be bought in a piece that you can grate yourself. If it is not available in this form, use the kind already grated and packaged in a round cardboard container.

**Spaghetti**  Dried spaghetti can be bought in any supermarket, and fresh spaghetti is now becoming more widely available. Use whichever you prefer.

**Tomatoes**  Cans of sweet Italian plum tomatoes are best for Italian cooking. If you are especially lucky, you may be able to find some fresh ones.

alian pasta has been troduced to many untries; here it is ade to look typically rman by being rved with nkfurters.

# INDEX

We would like to thank and acknowledge the following people for the use of their photographs and transparencies:

Anthony Blake Photo Library: 21; Bruce Coleman Ltd (Martini): T/Page, 9; (Mark N Boulton): 8; (Jessica Ehlers): 12; (Michael Klinec): 17; (Charles Henneghien): 19; Ebury Press: 17, 20, 24; Italian Trade Center: 10/11, 13, 14/15; Pasta Information Center: 12, 28; Pictures Color Library: 16, 26.